PAUSE 2 PRAISE

---

30 Days to Happier and Healthier Relationships with Your Adult Children

---

Lisa M. Swift-Young

DEDICATION

I give thanks and dedicate this book to my maternal grandmother, Alversa Williams Lee, and my paternal grandmother, Bernice Preyer Swift who held the light I followed into motherhood.

CONGRATULATIONS

You are on your way to happier and healthier relationships with your adult children. I want to set you up for success, so I have included two FREE resources to keep you and your tribe in track.

- **15 mediations sessions to keep you focused, courtesy of Headspace**

- **My personal playlist to keep you motivated and inspired, courtesy of Spotify**

Get FREE resources @
http://bit.ly/2pCmBJo

TABLE OF CONTENTS

FOREWORD

I am convinced that the purpose God brings two people together is the fruit their lives will produce. Children are certainly one manifestation of that fruit. Parenting presents joys and challenges and as children get older those increase. I remember when my daughter was born, I thought I would get a manual on what to do when we left the hospital. Nothing of that sort occurred. It became clear to my wife and I, as new parents that this would be on the job training. Watching our two children grow so fast creates a level of anxiety concerning our ability to maintain the relationship they will need from us as parents. Their needs will change, and it is important that parents remain relatable, responsible and reliable in the lives of their children.

Lisa Swift-Young has masterfully given us all a wonderful guidebook that helps us navigate the tough terrain of parenting our kids when they get older. This 30-day guide provides practical tools that help parents develop healthier relationships with their children. I believe when we are intentional about affirming our children and focusing on the blessing in them and around them, that we are in a better position to be who they need us to be. Nothing just happens. There has to be intentionality and connectivity. This book not only reinforces this idea naturally, but spiritually, as well.

This is a must read for anyone who truly wants to get it right and support their children as their dreams come to fruition. When we indulge in *Pause 2 Praise,* we are able to reflect and become refreshed. What we learn during this process is priceless. This book is a prayer answered and I pray it blesses and strengthens your relationships with your adult children and reignite your passion on what is possible when we *Pause 2 Praise.*

Bishop Joseph W. Walker, III,
Senior Pastor,
Mt. Zion Baptist Church (Nashville, TN)
Presiding Bishop,
Full Gospel Baptist Church Fellowship

PREFACE:

HOW THE PAUSE 2 PRAISE PRACTICE CHANGED MY LIFE

In the summer of 2016, I had an anxiety attack. I was still reeling from the sudden death of my Dad's youngest sister when my Mom's youngest sister had a massive stroke. Within a few weeks, an uncle was diagnosed with cancer and another aunt had a fatal heart attack. My husband had recently been laid off and my daughter had just moved more than 500 miles away to Detroit. My son, who lived more than 700 miles away in North Carolina, was wrestling with the challenges of corporate America. My community was mourning the murders of Philando Castile and Alton Sterling. The country was tearing itself apart in a divisive and demoralizing political meltdown. I was more than anxious about what would happen next.

My fear was becoming anxious. I began to pray for peace. I needed stability but I also wanted protection. I wanted to protect myself and my family from being swept up in the chaotic climate. I needed to put on the whole armor of God (Ephesians 6: 11-13 KJV).

Now as a working mother I was accustomed to being in control or at best, changing the circumstances toward my favor. I had excelled as a stellar sales and marketing professional for several major companies. On my self-directed "pause" from corporate into academia, I went from being an adjunct professor to a campus

3

president in just three years. So, I felt confident in my ability to assess a situation and develop a plan to make it better.

That July afternoon, as I sat in my car with my heart racing, body trembling, chest pounding, stomach-turning and breathing labored, I knew something was wrong. Although, I was literally parked in front of the emergency room preparing for my next call; I chose to Google my symptoms to self-diagnose my condition. I had all the symptoms of an anxiety attack.

The summer of 2016 taught me a lot. I was paralyzed with fear about many aspects concerning my immediate, extended family as well as society. I had been overwhelmed by the speed and intensity of the way things were evolving. I was becoming more anxious and losing my sense of stability. I needed peace. I knew I could not stop the barrage of negative images and rhetoric, but I could redirect my attention to the positive.

As a mother, I needed to protect my children. I felt responsible for finding a way to steady the ship, find that sweet spot in the eye of the storm where they and I would be safe. I knew that prayer was powerful, but I also knew that faith without works was dead (James 2:14-26 NIV). My interpretation was, if I wanted my prayers to manifest, I needed actions not just words.

The Pause 2 Praise practice was conceived. It empowered us to actively engage in steering the ship, navigating the negativity, and focusing on the positive. Pausing was the answer—stopping long enough to recognize what was always there. Praising the intrinsic beauty of each day and every person along the way. Partnering with my children to recognizing our own talents emerge from the shadows. This journey didn't start with a book in mind. It was simply a way for a mother to connect with her adult children. I never thought about where I was going. I just knew that I had to do something to change the tide. I knew there was power when we touch and agree. My prayer is that this journey will strengthen at least one relationship and reduce anxiety so you can live happier and build healthier relationships.

ACKNOWLEDGMENTS

My tribe:

My husband of 30 years, Antonio, who encouraged me to share my story. My favorite son, Brandon, and favorite daughter, Marissa, who indulged me and inspired me on this journey.

HOW TO BEST USE THIS BOOK

Pause 2 Praise Practice—Gather Your Tribe

Commitment and connection are the two most important components of this process. Commitment to making time to pause, to slow down and notice the abundance around you. There is a wealth of resources around us every day. In our fast-paced society, we often miss them because we are moving too fast for the next challenge. We are easily consumed with the next obstacle before we take a breath to celebrate. The fact is each day we are moving forward, getting stronger and becoming better.

Our drive to constantly move forward doesn't often make room for quiet reflection. It's hard to still yourself when media messages suggest that we have so much to do and not enough time to everything. We are often so preoccupied with the next trend, craze or fad that we rarely recognize our own needs. The laws of scarcity leave us feeling inundated and frustrated. Sometimes your commitment to practice is not enough to keep you on the path you want to be. That is where the connection will help you fill in the gap.

Humans are creatures of connections. We are wired to connect to one another. We are innately tribal. God created us to commune with one another. Being connected offers numerous health benefits, including increased feelings of belonging and purpose. Many studies note that human interactions increase levels of happiness, reduce levels of stress, and improve self-worth and confidence. We are born to crave closeness and if we don't get it, there are dire repercussions. We become anxious and unsettled. In extreme cases of solitude, we can even become mentally incapacitated.

The Pause 2 Praise practice accomplishes both commitment and connection. In our journey, my two adult children were my tribe. The benefits of doing this together are support and accountability. This practice is a guide for moms to connect with their adult children in a mature and meaningful way. In effect, forming a tribe that will share the same language and history of this experience. Referencing the scripture Matthew 18:19-20:

[19] "Again, truly I tell you that if two of you on earth agree about anything they ask for, it will be done for them by my Father in heaven. [20] For where two or three gathers in my name, there am I with them."

In this scripture, we discover the power of connection and gratitude. The practice will lead the tribe to live out the promises of Matthew 18:19-20. Bonding together to agree on gratitude and praise, sharing their insights and assessing their thoughts. Each morning will begin with an opportunity to begin in a more positive way. Reframing current mindsets and challenging perspectives of every day. Daily gratitude and praise will have benefits in every part of your life.

HOW IT WORKS

The Pause 2 Praise practice will help guide the tribe to take time each day to focus their energy toward each other and find ways to give praise and gratitude. Recognizing the abundant resources, the tribe and the individual can release their fears of scarcity and lean into the blessings of each new discovery. God's vision always comes with provision. The goal is to strengthen the connection that is positive and forward thinking. This foundation allows one to truly see the opportunities that were always there.

Using this daily practice, you and your tribe will feel more secure in the ways that count. More importantly, because of your commitment, you will unlock the power of connection and live happier and healthier.

Pause 2 Praise is a powerful practice that will help you see all the abundance in your life, and it will help you view your life totally different. It will only take five to ten minutes a day for the next thirty days, but the benefits will last a lifetime.

For the first nine days, we will talk specifically about resetting your mind, body and renewing your spirit. Of note, these three areas are foundational for growth and development.

Romans 12:2 says,

"Don't copy the behavior and customs of this world, but let God transform you into a new person by changing the way you think.

Then you will learn to know God's will for you, which is good and pleasing and perfect."

This renewing practice will help you recognize all the abundance that already exists at your core, your mind, body, and spirit.

The next twenty-one days are devoted to reestablishing physical and spiritual order. We will explore needs having to do with our natural desire for a predictable, orderly world. Seven areas of our lives which set the foundation for our sense of security and balance. Of note, the Bible recognizes seven as the number of completeness and achievement. Seven is the triumph of spirit over matter and taking the higher path of purpose. At the end of each day, there will be an activity to engage in the Pause 2 Praise practice.

Consequently, in just thirty days, you will have a testimony, unlike any other testimony. You and your tribe will see the blessings in your life and be able to enjoy the tangible and intangible experiences that were already there. You will also have a special connection to and with those who completed the journey with you. Moreover, you will have a greater understanding of who you are and who they are. This authentic journey will offer opportunities to use vulnerability as a pathway to exhibiting courage. Building a foundation for many more blessings to come.

Each day's objective is to give praise or gratitude for a specific encounter with God, someone or a new observation. Each step of the practice is detailed on the next few pages.

PAUSE 2 PRAISE - THE PRACTICE

P - The P simply stands for Pause. Commit to slow down, even for just five minutes a day, this will help you to see things more clearly instead of always in a blur.

A - Acknowledge, admire and appreciate. Oftentimes, we're going so fast that we never take the time to stop and acknowledge what is happening. Nor appreciate the opportunity of experience.

U - Unite is an essential part of the Pause to Praise practice. Find one or two people, preferably your tribe, other family members or close friends, to share this very intimate journey.

Matthew 18:19-20: Again, truly I tell you that if two of you on earth agree about anything they ask for, it will be done for them by my Father in heaven. For where two or three gathers in my name, there am I with them."

S - Stimulate conversation and share with your praise tribe your Pause 2 Praise moments. It doesn't have to take long, and this is where technology can benefit you. Use text messaging. As I mentioned in the beginning section, my children and I text every day and started with:

"Today I'm thankful for...." or "Today I'm grateful that.... "

That was enough for us to begin a dialogue and check in with each other.

"He who refreshes others will himself be refreshed." (Proverbs 11:25)

E - Evaluate. At the bottom of each page, there will be a scale that spells out the word, "Praise" with the letters P-R-A-I-S-E. Use the scale to circle the corresponding letter to denote how you feel each day after completing the Pause 2 Praise practice. Always feel free to circle more than one!!!

Today I feel

P   **R**   **A**   **I**   **S**   **E**

Positive   Relaxed   Accomplished   Inspired   Strong   Energized

RESTORE AND RENEW

The number three in the Bible is the number of divine wholeness, completeness, and perfection. If there ever was a desire to highlight an idea, thought, event or noteworthy figure in the Bible for its prominence, the number three was used to put a divine stamp of completion or fulfillment on the subject. Likewise, for the maximum benefit, the Pause 2 Praise practice is done in triplicate.

Each day, you will build familiarity and wholeness for resetting your mind, body, and spirit. You and your tribe will explore a deeper facet of each other and learned how to put away those thoughts and actions that distract you from noticing the opportunities for praise. Additionally, you will rediscovered the benefit of complete breathing and taken the time to explore your senses. Lastly, you will share an intimate encounter that strengthens and binds you together. As you and your tribe continue this journey, carry the lessons of the next nine days sessions with you. Moving forward, the following twenty-one days will help you and your tribe conquer common insecurities. You will find security and strength through synergy.

Ecclesiastes 4:12(ERV) says, "An enemy might be able to defeat one person, but two people can stand back-to-back to defend each other. And three people are even stronger. They are like a rope that has three parts wrapped together—it is very hard to break."

DAYS 1-3:

FREE YOUR MIND

Create the highest, grandest vision for your life, because you become what you believe

—Oprah Winfrey

The first part of this journey is to set the foundation for success. We will reset your mind, body, and spirit. We will spend three days in each area for a total of nine days. As with any journey, you need to pack or in this case unpack some baggage. Specifically, any person, place or thing that will distract, dissuade or, delay you from reaching your destination. Beginning this journey means letting go, uncluttering your mind, leaving a few habits behind, and making room to pick up a few skills along the way. I suggest making a voice recording of the fears and anxieties you want to unload and leave behind. Speak them into your voice recorder and put them on "Pause". If you prefer, write a letter detailing everything you want to unload. Each of the next nine days is dedicated to focusing on experiencing and feeling some basic things we take for granted every day.

We begin this journey with the end in mind. What do you want to feel, do or be at the end of this thirty-day journey? You determine your destiny. What type of life do you want for you and your adult children? This is about creating a mental vision of victory. What are you trying to achieve? It all begins in the mind. "Whether you think you can, or you think you can't, you are right"-(Henry Ford).

A familiar passage in Proverbs 23:7, declares "For as he **thinketh** in his heart, so is he."

It is a proven fact that we have the unique ability to use our minds to envision and create their future. The Secret, by Rhonda Byrne, proclaims that everything that comes into your life and everything that you experience does so through the magnetic power of thought. Our minds are truly the first step on the pathway to praise or peril. You set the course to your desired destination.

Day 1:

Today I am grateful for a mind that will create my new reality

As you reflect on today's gratitude prompt and chapter quote, what does it suggest you do differently?

Pause 2 Praise Practice

P - Pause and commit to slow down and breathe deeply.

A - Acknowledge the moment. Appreciate your right now.

U - Unite with your Praise Tribe. Connect via phone, text, email or in person.

S - Stimulate dialogue by sharing your thoughts.

E - Evaluate how today's reading/moment made you feel? (Circle all that apply)

P	**R**	**A**	**I**	**S**	**E**
Positive	Relaxed	Accomplished	Inspired	Strong	Energized

Notes to Self/Tribe:

Day 2:

Today I am grateful for a mind that will create my new reality

What is going to go well today? How will you contribute to your own happiness and joy today?

Pause 2 Praise Practice

P - Pause and commit to slow down and breathe deeply.

A - Acknowledge the moment. Appreciate your right now.

U - Unite with your Praise Tribe. Connect via phone, text, email or in person

S - Stimulate dialogue by sharing your thoughts.

E - Evaluate how today's reading/moment made you feel? (Circle all that apply)

P	**R**	**A**	**I**	**S**	**E**
Positive	Relaxed	Accomplished	Inspired	Strong	Energized

Notes to Self/Tribe:

Day 3:

Today I am grateful for a mind that will create my new reality

What are you grateful you learned in the past three days? How are you going to use what you learned moving forward?

Pause 2 Praise Practice

P - Pause and commit to slow down and breathe deeply.

A - Acknowledge the moment. Appreciate your right now.

U - Unite with your Praise Tribe. Connect via phone, text, email or in person.

S - Stimulate dialogue by sharing your thoughts.

E - Evaluate how today's activity/moment made you feel? (Circle all that apply)

P	R	A	I	S	E
Positive	Relaxed	Accomplished	Inspired	Strong	Energized

Notes to Self/ Tribe:

DAYS 4-6:

REFRESH YOUR BODY

One who has health has hope,
and one has hope has everything.

—**Arabic Proverb**

Some form of breathing is essential for most life forms. The simple act of inhaling oxygen and breathing out carbon dioxide is essential to how our planet exists. However, we often settle for short shallow breaths. Do we even remember what a deep breath feels like? Take the next sixty seconds to practice complete breathing.

1. *Inhale.* Using the diaphragm, inhale through your nose.

2. Smoothly and slowly, continue the inhalation by letting the chest expand.

3. Continue the inhalation until you cannot comfortably take in more air. Hold the breath for a few seconds and then...

4. *Exhale.* Slowly release your breath out through the mouth.

5. Continue the exhalation by letting the chest wall deflate. The belly collapses as the diaphragm moves upward, *pushing the air out of the lungs.*

Now that you've mastered this practice. Let's do it two more times. This time visualizing as you inhale all the goodness in your life. See positive coming to you. As you exhale, imagine all the anxiety, fear and negative thoughts blowing out and floating away.

Your body is a miraculous vessel. God gave us the ability to see, touch, taste, hear and smell. How often do you take time to be mindful of these gifts? Your heart beats through no conscious effort on your part. Spend today focusing and reacquainting yourself with your senses. *You are more than what you see in the mirror.* The complexities and the layers of your character are not present to the eyes; however, they shape you and develop your physical presentation. When you just see what is in front of you, you miss the nuances.

Today, experience life through your ears when you hear the wind and listen to the sound of water flowing in the shower. Through your nose, smell the air or sniff a flower. Through your hands and feet, feel the smoothness of your skin and the sensation of the ground against the soles of your feet. Today, use all your senses to explore the surrounding environment.

The reference to feet is particularly relevant to me because it was during an act of examining my feet, that I found two black spots on the soles of my feet. After several biopsies, they were categorized as abnormal but never conclusively cancer. The point is, our bodies send us signs and signals for ailments and diseases. However, we are often preoccupied and distracted.

The act of pausing allows you to activate all your senses so you can hear, touch, taste, smell, and receive the messages. Your body is uniquely designed for you. No one else will ever be just like you. Today Pause 2 Praise and give thanks to all that our bodies endure. Adore your vessel and give thanks.

Day 4:

Today I am thankful that I can see with more than my eyes

As you reflect on today's gratitude prompt and chapter quote, what does it suggest you see differently?

Pause 2 Praise Practice

P - Pause and commit to slow down and breathe deeply.

A - Acknowledge the moment. Appreciate your right now.

U - Unite with your Praise Tribe. Connect via phone, text, email or in person

S - Stimulate dialogue by sharing your thoughts.

E - Evaluate how today's reading/moment made you feel? (Circle all that apply)

P	**R**	**A**	**I**	**S**	**E**
Positive	Relaxed	Accomplished	Inspired	Strong	Energized

Notes to Self/ Tribe:

Day 5:

Today I am thankful that I can see with more than my eyes

What can you savor through each of your senses today (Think art, food, flowers or music)? How will you value your body today?

Pause 2 Praise Practice

P - Pause and commit to slow down and breathe deeply.

A - Acknowledge the moment. Appreciate your right now.

U - Unite with your Praise Tribe. Connect via phone, text, email or in person

S - Stimulate dialogue by sharing your thoughts.

E - Evaluate how today's reading/moment made you feel? (Circle all that apply)

P	R	A	I	S	E
Positive	Relaxed	Accomplished	Inspired	Strong	Energized

Notes to Self/ Tribe:

Day 6:

Today I am thankful that I can see with more than my eyes

What are 3-5 things you are thankful your body allows you to do?

Pause 2 Praise Practice

P - Pause and commit to slow down and breathe deeply.

A - Acknowledge the moment. Appreciate your right now.

U - Unite with your Praise Tribe. Connect via phone, text, email or in person

S - Stimulate dialogue by sharing your thoughts.

E - Evaluate how today's reading/moment made you feel? (Circle all that apply)

P	R	A	I	S	E
Positive	Relaxed	Accomplished	Inspired	Strong	Energized

Notes to Self/Tribe:

DAYS 7-9:

LET YOUR SPIRIT SOAR

My mission in life is not merely to survive, but to thrive; and to do so with some passion, some compassion, some humor, and some style.

—Maya Angelou

A nd God is able to bless you abundantly, so that in all things at all times, having all that you need, you will abound in every good work. (2 Corinthians 9:8 NIV)

God's will for us is to live in abundance. Yet, we lose hope at the slightest inconvenience. We resort to complaining about limited resources. When all we need to do is go to the Source to receive the resources.

I learned that lesson on a trip a few years ago. It was March 11, 2002, exactly six months after the World Trade Center disaster. I boarded a plane to New York City for a work trip just days after burying my mother-in-law. As we approached the World Trade Center site, the plane was silent as we paid our respects to our fallen Americans. I remember distinctly hearing a voice saying, "Do you trust me?" I knew immediately it wasn't a person, it was a Presence. After we landed, I learned that my luggage was missing. Mind you, this was a direct flight, so why was my luggage missing? It was Sunday afternoon, so everything had closed early. I didn't bring a carry-on, and I had a meeting the next morning with nothing to wear. I began to panic. This only added to my anxiety. I boarded the hotel shuttle while still on hold with the airlines to track down my luggage. I arrived at the hotel and checked in to my room. After some time, I learned my luggage was in Houston and would arrive the next morning. By this time, I was exhausted, overwhelmed, and hungry.

As I hung up the phone, I turned in amazement towards the bed. In my frazzled state, I had not noticed a white robe that was perfectly laid across my bed. Nor had I seen the fruit and cheese tray that was displayed on the nearby dresser. As I sank into the chair behind me, I realized what God was saying to me on the plane. *You don't need any of those things. I have everything you need. I can provide everything. If you trust me.* The truth is God provides for us every day. The Spirit went before me and prepared a place for me. God provided me with what I really needed that day and every day since then—food, clothing, shelter, and a good night's sleep.

Day 7:

Today I am grateful I am Spirit led and Spirit fed

Reflect on today's gratitude prompt and quote. What does it suggest that you see differently?

Pause 2 Praise Practice

P - Pause and commit to slow down and breathe deeply.

A - Acknowledge the moment. Appreciate your right now.

U - Unite with your Praise Tribe. Connect via phone, text, email or in person.

S - Stimulate dialogue by sharing your thoughts.

E - Evaluate how today's reading/moment made you feel? (Circle all that apply)

P	R	A	I	S	E
Positive	Relaxed	Accomplished	Inspired	Strong	Energized

Notes to Self/Tribe:

Day 8:

Today I am grateful I am Spirit-fed and Spirit-led

Think of a time when things didn't go the way you expected. What do you now see was the blessing in the lesson?

Pause 2 Praise Practice

P - Pause and commit to slow down and breathe deeply.

A - Acknowledge the moment. Appreciate your right now.

U - Unite with your Praise Tribe. Connect via phone, text, email or in person.

S - Stimulate dialogue by sharing your thoughts.

E - Evaluate how today's reading/moment made you feel? (Circle all that apply)

P	**R**	**A**	**I**	**S**	**E**
Positive	Relaxed	Accomplished	Inspired	Strong	Energized

Notes to Self/ Tribe:

Day 9:

Today I am grateful I am Spirit-fed and Spirit-led

What are you grateful you learned or did over the past nine days? How are you going to use it moving forward?

Pause 2 Praise Practice

P - Pause and commit to slow down and breathe deeply.

A - Acknowledge the moment. Appreciate your right now.

U - Unite with your Praise Tribe. Connect via phone, text, email or in person.

S - Stimulate dialogue by sharing your thoughts.

E - Evaluate how today's reading/moment made you feel? (Circle all that apply)

P	R	A	I	S	E
Positive	Relaxed	Accomplished	Inspired	Strong	Energized

Notes to Self/ Tribe:

CONQUER WITH CONFIDENCE

The next twenty-one days are designed to address feelings of insecurities and incompetence in key areas of life. Maslow's Hierarchy of Needs points to five foundational areas where one needs to feel confident in order to achieve self-actualization. We have already addressed the physiological needs in the previous part of the journey. This part of the journey deals with safety and security. Having a lack of confidence in these key areas often presents as fear and worry. Society is not always safe for women. Even more so for people of color. There is a constant barrage of messages and images that affirm our fragility. Whether it is real or perceived, fear and worry can prevent us from feeling happiness and joy. The next twenty-one days are about reframing your current situation and claiming praise in the present.

DAYS 10-12:

SPEAK POSITIVITY AND PROSPER

Such as I am, I am a precious gift.

—Zora Neale Hurston

One of my favorite quotes is *"If you can't change the people around you, change the people around you."* This simply means, if there are things or people that are keeping you from living your best life change them out for people or things that support your goals. Ultimately, you can choose to change your surroundings and limit your exposure to them. However, this doesn't work if *you* are the person you should stay away from. Often, we are our most hardened critic. Plainly stated, *the most fervent Enemy is usually the "Inner Me"*. Oftentimes, we think we must live with the hand we're dealt with. Self-limiting beliefs like this keep us from going after what we truly deserve. Change starts with changing your self- talk.

The messages we receive are the ones we send out. Need proof? Facebook, the popular social networking site, creates profiles on its users based on the user's input. Consequently, when users comment or like a negative post, the algorithm records this and begins to send them more of the same. Conversely, if users comment or like a positive post, the algorithm sends more positive messaging. Your feed is feeding you what you asked for. It's a la carte and you are ordering. Your click is a vote for more of the same.

Today, Pause 2 Praise yourself. Send yourself a message that you are worthy. I once heard someone state, *"You may not be able to control what you are fed; however, you are totally responsible for what you digest."* That goes for food as well as your thoughts. This is the ultimate, you are what you eat.

Today focus on your self-talk. Reward yourself speaking confidently about your gifts and talents. This is not arrogance, it is honoring the Giver and appreciating the gift. Make time today to compliment yourself and say positive things to yourself. Even my pastor often encourages himself during the sermon by proclaiming, "I'm doing the best I can."

More importantly, as you would a friend, forgive yourself for criticizing yourself. Apologize to yourself for negative, berating, or condescending self-talk.

Removing negative bias towards ourselves helps us to see our own beauty and makes it possible for us to notice the beauty in others. It is not about attaining someone else's concept of worth but embracing our own worth. *In a world where you can be anything, choose to appreciate who you are.* Here's a mantra you can practice from one of my favorite authors, Dr. Seuss. "Today you are You. That is truer than true. There is no one alive who is Youer than You."

Day 10:

Today I am grateful because no one will ever be able to do me like me

Reflect on today's gratitude prompt and quote. How does it make you feel?

Pause 2 Praise Practice

P - Pause and commit to slow down and breathe deeply.

A - Acknowledge the moment. Appreciate your right now.

U - Unite with your Praise Tribe. Connect via phone, text, email or in person.

S - Stimulate dialogue by sharing your thoughts.

E - Evaluate how today's reading/moment made you feel? (Circle all that apply)

P	**R**	**A**	**I**	**S**	**E**
Positive	Relaxed	Accomplished	Inspired	Strong	Energized

Notes to Self/Tribe:

Day 11:

Today I am grateful because no one will ever be able to do me like me

What are 3-5 strengths, talents, or gifts you are thankful for?

Pause 2 Praise Practice

P - Pause and commit to slow down and breathe deeply.

A - Acknowledge the moment. Appreciate your right now.

U - Unite with your Praise Tribe. Connect via phone, text, email or in person.

S - Stimulate dialogue by sharing your thoughts.

E - Evaluate how today's reading/moment made you feel? (Circle all that apply)

P	**R**	**A**	**I**	**S**	**E**
Positive	Relaxed	Accomplished	Inspired	Strong	Energized

Notes to Self/Tribe:

Day 12:

Today I am grateful because no one will ever be able to do me like me

What is going to go well today? How will you contribute to your own happiness and joy today?

Pause 2 Praise Practice

P - Pause and commit to slow down and breathe deeply.

A - Acknowledge the moment. Appreciate your right now.

U - Unite with your Praise Tribe. Check in on them.

S - Stimulate dialogue by sharing your thoughts.

E - Evaluate how today's reading/moment made you feel? (Circle all that apply)

P	**R**	**A**	**I**	**S**	**E**
Positive	Relaxed	Accomplished	Inspired	Strong	Energized

Notes to Self/Tribe:

DAYS 13-15:

MASTERPIECE IN THE MIRROR

To tell the truth is to become beautiful, to begin to love yourself, value yourself. And that's political, in its most profound way

—June Jordan

We are all awestruck when we see a spectacular sunrise or sunset. Do we also marvel when we look in the mirror? Are they not made by the same Creator? How is one often labeled as awesome and the other as awkward?

3 John 1:2 begins with a prayer:

"Dear Friend, I pray that you may enjoy good health and that all may go well with you, even as your soul is getting along well. "

Throw away pre-occupations and pre-packaged concepts of beauty imposed by society. Instead, learn to appreciate your body. See your body the way an artist would: as compositions of line, tone, form, light, and shadows. View your body as The Artist did. He created the majestic mountains and the vibrant valleys and then said this world needed one of you. Appreciate the fact that God meticulously designed your body using your ancestral DNA to craft the amazing person you see in the mirror today.

Like everything else that responds positively to praise and blessing, your body does, too. It is always beneficial to bless every part of your body with loving, positive thoughts and feelings, never disapproving the parts of your body that have decided to display their own individuality and not conform to social norms. A praised and blessed body is a happy body. *Your present body is a present from the Creator.* It is far better to praise it and take good care of it than to do otherwise. Body positivity is the practice of focusing on your outwardly positive qualities, skills, and talents.

Focus on appreciating and respecting what your body can do. As women, we don't always acknowledge and appreciate our bodies. Our bodies bring forth life. We were given unique padding and cushions to help us push back or push forward. The more we love ourselves, the more we can love others.

Recently, I was dining at an outdoor café and was privy to a conversation between two friends who were catching up. One of the ladies had a young girl about the age of eight with curly hair and mocha skin. As the ladies talked, the girl entertained herself by playing with her toys. One of her toys was a doll. During the conversation between the ladies, the mother's friend inquired about the doll. Immediately, the mother proclaimed the girl had chosen the doll herself and proudly explained that the girl was offered a doll that looked like her, but she had chosen a doll with straight hair and a snowy/ivory complexion instead of one in her own likeness. The mother then shared that the little girl thought this doll was prettier than she.

I wanted to tell her that although her doll was pretty, the doll would never be beautiful. The doll was produced thousands of times but, she was the original and only copy. That alone made her prettier. Moreover, she was smart, talented and kind, and adding that to pretty made her beautiful.

We can learn to admire the beauty of others, but we must avoid comparing or devaluing ourselves. Today remind yourself that media images are unrealistic and unattainable but what we see in the mirror is real and authentic. Everybody is somebody, but nobody has your body.

Day 13:

Today I am grateful I was divinely designed

As you reflect on today's gratitude prompt and chapter quote, what does it suggest you see differently?

Pause 2 Praise Practice

P - Pause and commit to slow down and breathe deeply.

A - Acknowledge the moment. Appreciate your right now.

U - Unite with your Praise Tribe. Connect via phone, text, email or in person.

S - Stimulate dialogue by sharing your thoughts.

E - Evaluate how today's reading/moment made you feel? (Circle all that apply)

P	**R**	**A**	**I**	**S**	**E**
Positive	Relaxed	Accomplished	Inspired	Strong	Energized

Notes to Self/Tribe:

Day 14:

Today I am grateful I was divinely designed

What do you appreciate about the way you look? How will you express your uniqueness today?

Pause 2 Praise Practice

P - Pause and commit to slow down and breathe deeply.

A - Acknowledge the moment. Appreciate your right now.

U - Unite with your Praise Tribe. Check in on them.

S - Stimulate dialogue by sharing your thoughts.

E - Evaluate how today's reading/moment made you feel? (Circle all that apply)

P	R	A	I	S	E
Positive	Relaxed	Accomplished	Inspired	Strong	Energized

Notes to Self/Tribe:

Day 15:

Today I am grateful I was divinely designed

What are you grateful you learned or did over the past 2 weeks? How are you going to use it moving forward?

Pause 2 Praise Practice

P - Pause and commit to slow down and breathe deeply.

A - Acknowledge the moment. Appreciate your right now.

U - Unite with your Praise Tribe. Connect via phone, text, email or in person.

S - Stimulate dialogue by sharing your thoughts.

E - Evaluate how today's reading/moment made you feel? (Circle all that apply)

P	**R**	**A**	**I**	**S**	**E**
Positive	Relaxed	Accomplished	Inspired	Strong	Energized

Notes to Self/Tribe:

DAYS 16-18:

CREATING YOUR KINGDOM ON EARTH

Look closely at the present you
are constructing, it should look like
the future you are dreaming.

—Alice Walker

"Thy kingdom come. Thy will be done on earth, as it is in heaven" Matthew 6:10 (KJV) This familiar passage in the Bible talks about how God wants His kingdom to be here on Earth as it is in heaven. So, let's spend a few minutes talking about your heaven. Visualize your heaven. What do you see? What colors do you see? What does it feel like? Is it hot or cold? What does it smell like? Is it a sun-drenched beach, or a lush tropical forest? How does this make you feel just thinking of this most perfect place? What are some ways you would describe it? Relaxing, stress-free, or joyful? Now, look around. Do you get that same feeling where you are right now? Why or Why not? When you looked around, did you see chaos? Papers, clothing, or dishes piled up?

Manifest your kingdom on earth. Take the vision of this place that made you safe, comfortable and relaxed and creates that space in your home. It can be an entire room or a closet, like in the Christian drama, "The War Room."

Another idea is offered by the BET series *Being Mary Jane*. The lead character used sticky notes to leave words of encouragement to herself. Things to remind herself of her talents and all her abilities to inspire, empower, and ground her. You could do the same, grab some sticky notes and write notes to yourself. Put them on the wall. Put them on the mirror. Place them so they are visible multiple times throughout the day, maybe before you head out the door, or maybe before you go to bed for a peaceful sleep. Do this to create an environment that reflects your kingdom on earth. Any place you can sit and be at peace to gather your thoughts. This is about creating your heaven on earth. A physical place you can go every day that makes you feel safe, happy, and joyful. This will reset your day, your week, and the rest of your life.

Day 16:

Today I am thankful I have a place of peace

Reflect on today's gratitude prompt and quote. What does it suggest that you do differently?

Pause 2 Praise Practice

P - Pause and commit to slow down and breathe deeply.

A - Acknowledge the moment. Appreciate your right now.

U - Unite with your Praise Tribe. Connect via phone, text, email or in person.

S - Stimulate dialogue with your thoughts.

E - Evaluate how today's reading/moment made you feel? (Circle all that apply)

P	**R**	**A**	**I**	**S**	**E**
Positive	Relaxed	Accomplished	Inspired	Strong	Energized

Notes to Self/Tribe:

Day 17:

Today I am thankful
I have a place of peace

What is going to go well today? How will you contribute to your own happiness and joy today?

Pause 2 Praise Practice

P - Pause and commit to slow down and breathe deeply.

A - Acknowledge the moment. Appreciate your right now.

U - Unite with your Praise Tribe. Check in on them.

S - Stimulate dialogue by sharing your thoughts.

E - Evaluate how today's reading/moment made you feel? (Circle all that apply)

P	**R**	**A**	**I**	**S**	**E**
Positive	Relaxed	Accomplished	Inspired	Strong	Energized

Notes to Self/ Tribe:

Day 18:

Today I am thankful
I have a place of peace

What are the 3-5 things you like about your current environment? How will you do to make it better moving forward?

Pause 2 Praise Practice

P - Pause and commit to slow down and breathe deeply.

A - Acknowledge the moment. Appreciate your right now.

U - Unite with your Praise Tribe. Check in on them.

S - Stimulate dialogue by sharing your thoughts.

E - Evaluate how today's reading/moment made you feel? (Circle all that apply)

P	**R**	**A**	**I**	**S**	**E**
Positive	Relaxed	Accomplished	Inspired	Strong	Energized

Notes Self/ Tribe:

DAYS 19-21:

BUILDING AND BONDING

You can't have relationships with other people until you give birth to yourself.

—Sonia Sanchez

One of the areas that I felt the most vulnerable was in my personal relationship with my adult children. The dynamics of our relationship was changing. I could no longer shield them from hurt and harm. I had to accept the fact that they would engage in situations and environments that I wouldn't be able to manage. This led me to worry, which ultimately led me to fear and a loss of security. I was completely confident in their ability to navigate through life, it was the "others" that concerned me. I had to trust that God was in control of any forces that would come against them. Accepting things, I could not change gave me the courage to change the things I could.

I chose harness what author Brene Brown refers to as *The Power of Vulnerability* and use it to build my courage. It was no longer my job to protect them and shield them. My role was to be a mentor, or as my husband says, be a life coach. Earnestly listening to them and willingly learning from them. I began to share the obstacles I had faced in my career and in my own personal development. I shared things that I am still struggling with and have yet to overcome. They began to see me for who I am. A woman who is still learning and growing. I didn't hide the flaws. I challenged myself to see them for who they were and not who I wanted them to be.

They began to share their concerns and frustrations. We began to confer and consult on how we could work together as a family to build up ourselves and help others. As a result, we established a donor-advised fund to support financial literacy for underserved populations. This would not have been possible without the Pause 2 Praise practice. Our daily practice allowed us to reframe problems into possibilities and ultimately create opportunities to help others prosper.

Day 19:

Today I am grateful I have more bonds than boundaries

Reflect on today's gratitude prompt and quote. What does it suggest that you do differently?

Pause 2 Praise Practice

P - Pause and commit to slow down and breathe deeply.

A - Acknowledge the moment. Appreciate your right now.

U - Unite with your Praise Tribe. Connect via phone, text, email or in person.

S - Stimulate dialogue by sharing your thoughts.

E - Evaluate how today's reading/moment made you feel? (Circle all that apply)

P	R	A	I	S	E
Positive	Relaxed	Accomplished	Inspired	Strong	Energized

Notes Self/Tribe:

Day 20:

Today I am grateful I have more bonds than boundaries.

Think of a time when things didn't go the way you expected. What do you now see was the blessing in the lesson?

Pause 2 Praise Practice

P - Pause and commit to slow down and breathe deeply.

A - Acknowledge the moment. Appreciate your right now.

U - Unite with your Praise Tribe. Connect via phone, text, email or in person.

S - Stimulate dialogue by sharing your thoughts.

E - Evaluate how today's reading/moment made you feel? (Circle all that apply)

P	**R**	**A**	**I**	**S**	**E**
Positive	Relaxed	Accomplished	Inspired	Strong	Energized

Notes to Self/Tribe:

Day 21:

Today I am grateful I have more bonds than boundaries

What are 3-5 strengths, talents, or gifts you are thankful for?

Pause 2 Praise Practice

P - Pause and commit to slow down and breathe deeply.

A - Acknowledge the moment. Appreciate your right now.

U - Unite with your Praise Tribe. Connect via phone, text, email or in person.

S - Stimulate dialogue by sharing your thoughts.

E - Evaluate how today's reading/moment made you feel? (Circle all that apply)

P	**R**	**A**	**I**	**S**	**E**
Positive	Relaxed	Accomplished	Inspired	Strong	Energized

Notes to Self/Tribe:

DAYS 22-24:
MIND OVER MONEY

The most common way people give up their power is by thinking they don't have any.

—Alice Walker

We often associate having resources with having money. The way we perceive money often defines who we are and what we have. Our culture places supreme value on pursuing, acquiring and spending money. So, consciously or unconsciously, we ask for more. Covertly or overtly using it to validate our worth to ourselves and our peers. Rarely are we thankful for what we have before we ask for more? Honestly, I have more shoes that I can wear and have bought more clothes because they were on sale than I will ever wear. Although these purchases made me feel better in the moment, it was short lived. In fact, a recent study showed the "Halo effect" entices us to buy more to get the same feeling again. This leaves way too many people trying to find happiness in the mall or through shopping.

So, how can we overcome our insecurities around money and use it to bring us joy and happiness? Praise, plan and prosper.

We find ourselves in trouble financially by not managing the resources we already have. God promises that being faithful over a few things, He will make you ruler over many (Matthew 25:23, KJV). Successfully managing over our resource is an important step in regaining our power to overcome our insecurities about money. Telling your money where to go instead of it telling you where to go is being in control. Viewing budgeting as a way of telling your money where to go was a game changer for me. Instead of it controlling us, we are controlling it. Our ancestors knew how to budget. My maternal grandparents raised fourteen children on the salary of a part-time barber and laborer. They managed to find the finances and resources in the deep south of the 40s and the 50s to raise all fourteen of them to adulthood. Proverbs 31:14 -16 speaks of a woman that handles her finances and knows the value of investing for the future. These verses offer an example of how one can manage finances, appreciate the fruits of their labor, and share with others by appropriately managing their finances.

I am supremely thankful that my father was adamant about saving. He learned this lesson from Aunt Essie, my great-aunt. Her mantra was, "Always pay yourself first." Always set aside something for you and your family. Pause and pay yourself first. Make a point to put aside a dime out of every dollar. Be consistent, and you will find that you will build a nest egg that will carry you through.

Share your knowledge with your tribe. My family took an online course, Financial Peace, a Word-based program that talks specifically about managing finances. Today, I am thankful for the information we learned together. My husband and I were able to have some very open conversations with our children about money and how we would like for things to be handled. There is a great amount of peace and joy when we have control over our finances. It doesn't matter if you are managing $400 a week or $8,000 a month. Invest in your family and your future. Conquering fears about finances helped us have healthier conversations which led to a happier life. Doing these two things prepares your family for a harvest that will allow you to share your knowledge and treasures with all that are connected to you. Pause, Plan and your family will Prosper.

Day 22:

Today I gratefully choose God's purpose over my plan

Reflect on today's gratitude prompt and quote. What do they suggest that you do differently?

Pause 2 Praise Practice

P - Pause and commit to slow down and breathe deeply.

A - Acknowledge the moment. Appreciate your right now.

U - Unite with your Praise Tribe. Connect via phone, text, email or in person.

S - Stimulate dialogue by sharing your thoughts.

E - Evaluate how today's reading/moment made you feel? (Circle all that apply)

P	**R**	**A**	**I**	**S**	**E**
Positive	Relaxed	Accomplished	Inspired	Strong	Energized

Notes to Self/Tribe:

Day 23:

Today I gratefully choose God's purpose over my plan

Studies show that giving boosts happiness more than spending. How can you share your resources today?

Pause 2 Praise Practice

P - Pause and commit to slow down and breathe deeply.

A - Acknowledge the moment. Appreciate your right now.

U - Unite with your Praise Tribe. Connect via phone, text, email or in person.

S - Stimulate dialogue by sharing your thoughts.

E - Evaluate how today's reading/moment made you feel? (Circle all that apply)

P	**R**	**A**	**I**	**S**	**E**
Positive	Relaxed	Accomplished	Inspired	Strong	Energized

Notes to Self/Tribe:

Day 24:

Today I gratefully choose God's purpose over my plan

What are the 3-5 things you have learned over the past 3 weeks? How will you use them moving forward?

Pause 2 Praise Practice

P - Pause and commit to slow down and breathe deeply.

A - Acknowledge the moment. Appreciate your right now.

U - Unite with your Praise Tribe. Connect via phone, text, email or in person.

S - Stimulate dialogue by sharing your thoughts.

E - Evaluate how today's reading/moment made you feel? (Circle all that apply)

P	**R**	**A**	**I**	**S**	**E**
Positive	Relaxed	Accomplished	Inspired	Strong	Energized

Notes Self/ Tribe:

DAYS 25-27:
GIFTS AND TALENTS @ WORK

"People who work hard often work too hard ..
May we learn to honor the hammock, the
siesta, the nap and the pause in all its forms."

—Alice Walker

This chapter will address how worrying about our employment affects our praise and faith. We often focus on what our jobs are not and rarely acknowledge what they are. At the base level, our careers offer a way for us to be remunerated for our time. At the median level, it is the way we use our talents. At the highest level, it is the way that we use our time, develop our talent, and are compensated financially while contributing to society in a meaningful way.

Many times, our jobs frame our sense of worthiness to a team, an organization or a community. Most are aware of the recent job market challenges in the US. Unfortunately, many are also consumed by uncontrollable like layoffs, economic trends, and restructuring. I know firsthand the harsh realities of a volatile employment environment. My corporate career in pharmaceuticals was marked with takeovers, right-sizing, and mergers. Each one left me waiting by the phone to see if I would have a job the next day. Even when I took a self-directed career pause to explore academia, I found myself in a similar situation when the college "regrouped" under new management.

What I learned was that shifts were inevitable for sifting. These changes built my resilience, increased my resolve and kept my skills sharp. When I landed at the next position, I saw things differently and focused on those things I could improve. Learning new things gave me the confidence to write this book. My son and daughter seized opportunities to leverage their work skills to pursue entrepreneurial ventures.

The simple act of accepting and receiving praise will make your time at work more enjoyable and have better work experiences. Moreover, I found that I received more joy at the moment and spent less time worrying. Additionally, studies have found that praise can help you learn more. Fully examine the opportunities to learn more about your position or inquire about the work of others. Praising someone else's expertise and skills has a residual effect on your own mood. Especially on the days where you are overwhelmed and challenged. This is a good opportunity to practice and remember Colossians 1:11. "Strengthened with all might, according to his glorious power, unto all patience and longsuffering with joyfulness."

This is the perfect opportunity to acknowledge and Pause 2 Praise. Celebrate the fact that today, you stayed the course and practiced self-control. Two valuable lessons are applicable to many of life's trials and triumphs.

Day 25:

Today I am grateful I can use life's blocks as my building blocks.

Reflect on today's gratitude prompt and quote. What does it suggest that you see differently?

Pause 2 Praise Practice

P - Pause and commit to slow down and breathe deeply.

A - Acknowledge the moment. Appreciate your right now.

U - Unite with your Praise Tribe. Connect via phone, text, email or in person.

S - Stimulate dialogue by sharing your thoughts.

E - Evaluate how today's reading/moment made you feel? (Circle all that apply)

P	**R**	**A**	**I**	**S**	**E**
Positive	Relaxed	Accomplished	Inspired	Strong	Energized

Notes to Self/ Tribe:

Day 26:

Today I am grateful I can use life's blocks as my building blocks.

How did/will you value your talents, skills, or gifts today?

Pause 2 Praise Practice

P - Pause and commit to slow down and breathe deeply.

A - Acknowledge the moment. Appreciate your right now.

U - Unite with your Praise Tribe. Connect via phone, text, email or in person.

S - Stimulate dialogue by sharing your thoughts.

E - Evaluate how today's reading/moment made you feel? (Circle all that apply)

P	**R**	**A**	**I**	**S**	**E**
Positive	Relaxed	Accomplished	Inspired	Strong	Energized

Notes to Self/Tribe:

Day 27:

Today I am grateful I can use life's blocks as my building blocks.

What are the 3-5 things you like about your current environment? How will you make it better moving forward?

Pause 2 Praise Practice

P - Pause and commit to slow down and breathe deeply.

A - Acknowledge the moment. Appreciate your right now.

U - Unite with your Praise Tribe. Connect via phone, text, email or in person.

S - Stimulate dialogue by sharing your thoughts.

E - Evaluate how today's reading/moment made you feel? (Circle all that apply)

P	**R**	**A**	**I**	**S**	**E**
Positive	Relaxed	Accomplished	Inspired	Strong	Energized

Notes to Self/ Tribe:

DAYS 28-30:

WHAT A WONDERFUL WORLD

The miracle of your existence
calls for celebration every day.

—Oprah Winfrey

How often do we pay attention to the order of nature? How thunder announces the coming of rain. The sound of wind rustling through the leaves on the trees. How seasons effortlessly transition on cue? Nature offers a myriad of opportunities to offer praise. If only we would pause to appreciate the beauty around us. God designed Earth with specifically the right concentration of hydrogen and oxygen to sustain human life. The ecosystem has a perfect balance of nutrients and resources for self-sustainability. While we whizz by in our planes, trains, and automobiles, we often miss the subtle transitions. We are consumed with tapping on our phones, binge-watching television shows, and listening to endless chatter. This frantic, hectic pace makes us anxious, stressed and overwhelmed. We miss the flowers blooming and the raindrops bouncing on the water. We rarely notice that above the clouds, there are always blue skies.

For the total eclipse of 2018, I paused long enough to appreciate how every fifty or so years, nature speeds up the process and leaves all of us to marvel at its synchronized flow. I was astonished to witness day turn into night and night turn into day. What normally takes twenty-four hours, occurred in less than two minutes! As the moon began to cover the sun, darkness followed along with the sound of crickets, and the appearance of gnats dancing in the streetlights. The hot sun gave way to a cool breeze that caused a chill to blanket the lawn. Then came total darkness, and all was still. Within a matter of seconds, the sun began to shine through. The birds began to chirp, and the streetlights began to dim. The darkness receded and daylight prevailed bringing the warmth of the sun.

The media described it as a miracle of nature and a sight to behold. A once in a lifetime occurrence. But here is the secret, this miracle happens every day. We generally don't pay attention to the signs and wonders around us. The opportunities to engage with nature, all while appreciating the calm in the chaos. Recognizing that regardless of the circumstances or situations, nature keeps its order. Accomplishing what it set out to do. It stays focused on its purpose. Pausing 2 Praise allows us to capture those moments and gain insight and inspiration from our environment.

Day 28:

Today I am thankful that miracles are proof that God is still moving

As you reflect on today's gratitude prompt and chapter quote, what does it suggest you see differently?

Pause 2 Praise Practice

P - Pause and commit to slow down and breathe deeply.

A - Acknowledge the moment. Appreciate your right now.

U - Unite with your Praise Tribe. Connect via phone, text, email or in person.

S - Stimulate dialogue by sharing your thoughts.

E - Evaluate how today's reading/moment made you feel? (Circle all that apply)

P	**R**	**A**	**I**	**S**	**E**
Positive	Relaxed	Accomplished	Inspired	Strong	Energized

Notes to Self/ Tribe:

Day 29:

Today I am thankful that miracles are proof that God is still moving

How will you savor something in your environment today?

Pause 2 Praise Practice

P - Pause and commit to slow down and breathe deeply.

A - Acknowledge the moment. Appreciate your right now.

U - Unite with your Praise Tribe. Check in on them.

S - Stimulate dialogue by sharing your thoughts.

E - Evaluate how today's reading/moment made you feel? (Circle all that apply)

P	**R**	**A**	**I**	**S**	**E**
Positive	Relaxed	Accomplished	Inspired	Strong	Energized

Notes to Self/ Tribe:

Day 30:

Today I am thankful that miracles are proof that God is still moving

What are the 3-5 things you learned over the past 30 days? How will you use them moving forward?

Pause 2 Praise Practice

P - Pause and commit to slow down and breathe deeply.

A - Acknowledge the moment. Appreciate your right now.

U - Unite with your Praise Tribe. Check in on them.

S - Stimulate dialogue by sharing your thoughts.

E - Evaluate how today's reading/moment made you feel? (Circle all that apply)

P	**R**	**A**	**I**	**S**	**E**
Positive	Relaxed	Accomplished	Inspired	Strong	Energized

Notes to Self/ Tribe:

PAUSE 2 PRAISE:

CALM IN THE EYE OF LIFE'S STORMS

"Every small positive change
we make in ourselves repays us in
confidence in the future."

—Alice Walker

This book was a guide for moms to connect with their adult children in a mature and meaningful way. The goal was to form a connection that was positive and forward thinking. I hope this book helped you to take time each day to focus your energy toward the positive. Every three days, we shifted our focus to overcome our basic need for security while recognizing opportunities for personal, familiar, environment, employment, and mental growth. Releasing fear and leaning into the blessings. The Pause 2 Praise practice clears the chaos, encouraging one to truly see the opportunities that were always there. We have reached a milestone in this part of the journey.

I started this practice to create calm in the chaos of the summer of 2016. I once took a defensive driving course that taught me to acknowledge the obstacles on the road but look in the direction you want to go. Similarly, I could not stop what was happening, but I could steer myself and my children away from the proverbial cliff. You and your tribe have also avoided the cliff and redirected your path toward a more authentic relationship. Take time to reflect on the journey. Pause and think about the stories you have shared. The knowledge that has flowed between you and your tribe. For us, the Pause 2 Praise practice has been a way for us to see the challenges but champion solutions.

Over the past three years, many things have changed. Some were trials others were triumphs. There was the loss of a beloved aunt and uncle. The dissolution of a marriage and a career transition, as well as the birth of children and the birth of several businesses. We have traveled to East Africa and have explored Havana. Each experience, we faced it together. We made the time to share our daily praises through them all. We manifested the relationship we wanted and believed in the power of Matthew 18:19-20.

Again, truly I tell you that if two of you on earth agree about anything they ask for, it will be done for them by my Father in heaven. For where two or three gathers in my name, there am I with them.

We traded hurting for healing and gained a healthier and happier relationship. We stopped worrying about 'what if' and started living in 'what is.' We found that working toward our goals was more profitable and beneficial than worrying about our future.

Peter 5: 7 "Cast all your cares to him because he cares for you."

Storms in life are imminent and some storms give way to tornadoes. After a little research, I learned something new and interesting about the composition of tornadoes that relates to our experience. We are all familiar with the large ominous tornado funnel structure that evokes fear of the impending destruction. It is also commonly known that the eyewall is the epicenter of its destructive nature. However, it was recently discovered that when you are at the center of a tornado, the eye, and look up, there is peace and serenity. The skies are blue, and the sun shines bright.

So, the next time life's storms or tornadoes threaten to toss you and your tribe around, Pause 2 Praise. Stay close together and move with the storm by practicing the tools you learned over the past 30 days to stay in the eye. Look up, you will see that God has His Eye on you.

CONGRATULATIONS

You finished the first 30 days of "Pause 2 Praise".

I truly appreciate you for taking me along on this journey. I hope you enjoyed it and will continue to benefit from the experience.

Could you give me your feedback?

I would really appreciate it if you left a review on Amazon. It helps others find out about the Pause 2 Praise practice.

RESOURCES

If you desire more resources for motivation and gratitude prompts:

<u>Daily motivation</u>

Follow "Pause 2 Praise" on Facebook and/or "pause2praisebooks" on Instagram.

<u>Need to practice" Pausing".</u>

I'll sent you 15 **FREE meditation exercises**

<u>Need to stay motivated</u>

I'll send you my personal Spotify playlist

Get FREE resources @
http://bit.ly/2pCmBJo

ABOUT THE AUTHOR

Lisa has realized personal milestones as a Christian, wife, cousin, sister, coach, and friend. Professionally, Lisa has excelled in many positions and held numerous titles. Account Manager, Executive Sales Consultant, Sales Trainer, Campus President, Professor, and Dean to name a few. All these roles combine and equip her to embrace her most challenging, consuming, and character-building role: Mom.

She and her husband of 30 years have been blessed to raise two incredible self-sufficient adults. A favorite son and a favorite daughter. In addition to her immediate family, she is deeply committed and connected to her expansive extended family. She credits her tribe with continuously inspiring her to become her best self.

In her most current project, Pause 2 Praise, she shares a particularly turbulent period with her immediate and extended family. She recounts how her personal and professional skills merged to liberate and elevate her family.

Made in the USA
San Bernardino, CA
18 November 2019